Also by Maureen Roffey

How Many?
What's the Weather?
How Do We Get There?
Home Sweet Home
Look, There's My Hat!

Copyright © 1995 by Maureen Roffey
All rights reserved.
The right of Maureen Roffey to be identified as
the author of this work has been asserted
by her in accordance with the Copyright,
Designs and Patents Act 1988.
This edition first published in Great Britain in 1995
by Macmillan Children's Books, a division of
Macmillan Publishers Limited, Cavaye Place,
London SW10 and Basingstoke and
associated companies worldwide.

ISBN 0 333 58275 6 (hb)
ISBN 0 333 59206 9 (pb)

A CIP catalogue record for this book is
available from the British Library.
Printed in Singapore.

What's the Time?

Maureen Roffey

MACMILLAN CHILDREN'S BOOKS

What is the time?

Time to get dressed.

What is the time?

Time for breakfast.

What is the time?

eleven o'clock

What is the time?

What is the time?

It is dressing-up time.

What is the time?

six o'clock   It is bathtime.

seven o'clock
It is bedtime.

Sleep tight!